R. Finnegan & J. Wiles
IRISH GOVERNMENT PUBLICATIONS

Richard Finnegan is Director of Irish Studies
and Professor of Political Science at Stonehill
College in Massachusetts. James Wiles is Pro-
fessor of Economics at Stonehill College and
Director of the College's Irish Government
Documents Project.

Irish Government Publications

A Select List 1972–1992

RICHARD B. FINNEGAN &
JAMES L. WILES

IRISH ACADEMIC PRESS

This book was typeset
in 10 on 12 Times by
Carrigboy Typesetting Services for
IRISH ACADEMIC PRESS
Kill Lane, Blackrock, Co. Dublin, Ireland

and in North America
IRISH ACADEMIC PRESS
C/o ISBS, 5804 NE Hassalo St, Portland, OR 97213

A catalogue record for this book
is available from the British Library.

ISBN 0–7165–2524–0

Printed in Great Britain by
Cambridge University Press, Cambridge

Preface

The authors are grateful for all the help they have received in putting this reference work together. The initial typing of the lists into the computer at Stonehill was done by Karlene Mulcahey and Mary Malone, student assistants to the Irish Studies Program. In checking and cross checking the lists we had the patient and constant assistance of Freda MacLeod. Additional help on the preparation of the data base was provided by Margaret Myers of the Library and James Burns of the Computer Center. Donna Benoit provided, as she has done in the past, absolutely invaluable assistance in preparing the text for publication. The Academic Dean of the College provided financial support to bring a disparate collection of lists into a coherent manuscript. Finally we want to thank Michael Adams of Irish Academic Press for being receptive to the idea of publishing an updated select list and his help in bringing it to fruition.

This volume represents another project in the collaboration of the authors who together have created the Archive of Irish Government Official Publications at Stonehill College. This Archive is the only comprehensive collection of Irish Government Official Publications in the United States. While working on the completion of the Archive we published *Aspirations and Realities: A Documentary History of Economic Development Policy in Ireland since 1922.* (Greenwood Press, Westport, CT., 1993) which was based upon Official Publications in the Archive. Stonehill's President, Bartley MacPhaidin, has been unstinting in his support of the Irish Studies Program, of the work on the Official Publications Archive and the publication of this book. We can only wish other scholars such good fortune.

Richard B. Finnegan

James L. Wiles

Contents

5   Preface

9   Introduction

11 SELECT LIST

11   Government

18   Political and Economic Relations with the EC

22   National Finance

23   Money and Monetary Policy

23   Agriculture Food and Forestry

24   Economic Policy: Development Planning and Trade

31   Transportation, Energy and the Environment

32   Status of Women

33   Labour

34   Social Service and Security

35   Health

37   Education

38   National Culture

39   Legal Administration, Police, Law

43 Select List of Serials

49 Publications of the National Economic and Social Council

53 Index

Introduction

This work builds upon the foundation of the volume prepared by Percy and Grace Ford, *Select List of Reports and Inquiries of the Irish Dail and Senate 1922–1972* (Irish University Press, Dublin, 1974) and Arthur Maltby and Brian McKenna's volume, *Irish Official Publications: A Guide to the Republic of Ireland Papers, with a Breviate of Reports 1922–1972* (Oxford, Pergamon Press, 1980). These two volumes provide guides to Irish Official Publications which are of critical value to the researcher in that five decades of Official Publications are classified topically. The materials include a select list of departmental reports, commissions, special inquiries and parliamentary reports. Additionally Maltby and McKenna also provide a breviate, or summary, of the key ideas in the reports and included a comprehensive list of all the serials published by the Stationary Office and other agencies. Both volumes cover the same period, the first fifty years of the Irish state.

The genesis of this volume was in the creation of a collection of Irish Official Publications at Stonehill College. The authors of this work, in seeking to identify those materials that should be in the collection, noted the absence of a reference work covering the period from 1972 to 1992. The only source available to the researcher is the annual Stationary Office Catalogues which indicate what has been published by that office, classified by departments. While not devoid of utility the lack of integration across the years and the lack of an index make the catalogues a clumsy research tool. The completion of the collection of Irish Official Publications at Stonehill College in 1993 provided an opportunity to prepare this guide as a companion to the Fords and Maltby and McKenna volumes.

Like its predecessors the book provides a selective, but comprehensive, list of Official Publications. These are listed topically and then chronologically within the category or sub-category. The work also includes an index to assist the reader. It differs from its predecessors in that while the organizing topics are very similar to the Fords and Maltby and McKenna, categories had to be added to account for the emergence of government papers and reports on such items as the status of women, the environment, and the European Community. Our work differs from the Fords in that a comprehensive list of serials is included in that so much valuable material for the researcher is in the form of annual reports and year end summaries.

The introduction to Maltby and McKenna provides a detailed explanation of the different types of Official Publications. This book confines itself to those publications issued by the Stationary Office. While this constitutes the vast majority of Irish government papers, it is not inclusive of some reports issued by the Central Bank, by government departments themselves and those issued by State Sponsored bodies such as the Electricity Supply Board, The Law Reform Commission, or Radio Telefis Eireann. The researcher must take care to note the movement of a civil service agency to the status of a State Sponsored Body, such as the Industrial Development Authority, which can change the source of publications. Moreover as noted above the list is selective in that materials of a narrow and technical nature are excluded. The goal was to provide the user with the papers which track the major areas of domestic policy. While selective the authors sought to err on the side of inclusion rather than exclusion.

The dates and call numbers of publications deserve some comment. The date that a paper was completed can differ from the year that it was published by the Stationary Office. While not common it requires a choice and, like the Fords and Maltby and McKenna, the date used in this work is the date of publication by the Stationary Office. The Stationary Office also assigns a catalogue number to every document. The letter at the beginning of the number represents the Department and the numbers following identify the type of publication from that source and, if a serial, an additional number gives the place of that particular item in the series. All publications in this volume use the numbers assigned by the Stationary Office. There is an additional number called the Presentation number for papers that have been 'presented' before the Dail and/or Seanad. This number is not given in this volume as it has little practical use and, as all the documents do not have them, is not a uniform identifying feature.

The department issuing the publication gives a significant clue as to its place-ment in the topical select list. While a significant clue, it may not be sufficient. The items are listed once in the volume and the placement can often be an arbitrary matter as papers can legitimately fit into several categories. The authors sought to locate the placement by the central thrust of the document's material and not merely by the words of the title. The index, however, provides the reader with a cross reference to the topics covered in the papers.

Select List

GOVERNMENT

Elections

1973	M.51/9	Election Results and Transfer of Votes in General Election, February, 1973, for Twentieth Dail
1975	K.110	Local Elections, 1974—Results and Statistics, February, 1975
1978	PP7/1	Seanad General Election, August 1977 and Bye-Elections to 1973–77 Seanad
1978	M51/10	Election Results and Transfer of Votes in General Election (June, 1977) for Twenty-First Dail
1980	K123	Results of Presidential Elections and Referenda 1937–1979. (With notes on the electoral and polling procedures)
1981	M51/11	Election Results and Transfer of Votes in General Election (June, 1981) for Twenty-Second Dail and Bye-Elections to Twenty-First Dail (1977–1981)
1982	M51/12	Election results and transfer of votes in General election (February 1982) for twenty-third Dail
1982	PP7/2	Seanad General Election, August 1981 and Bye-Elections to 1977–81 Seanad
1982	PP7/3	Seanad General Election, April 1982
1983	K130	Report of the Working Party on the Register of Electors— March 1983
1983	M51/13	Election Results and Transfer of votes in General Election (November 1982) for Twenty-Fourth Dail and Bye-election to Twenty-third Dail (March–November, 1982)
1985	K123/1	Results of Presidential Elections and Referenda, 1937–1984
1987	M51/14	Election Results and Transfer Votes in General Election (February 1987) for Twenty-Fifth Dail and Bye-Elections to Twenty-Fourth Dail (1982–1987)
1988	PP7/5	Seanad General Election, April 1987
1990	M/51/15	Election Results and Transfer of Votes in General Election (June, 1989) for Twenty-Sixth Dail
1990	P/P/07/006	Seanad General Election, August 1989 and Bye-Election to 1987/89 Seanad
1992	K/154	Local Elections, 1991

1992	K/156	Toghchain Uachtarain 1938–1990
		Presidential Elections 1938–1990
1992	K/157	Reifrinn in Eireann 1937–1987. Referenda in Ireland 1937–1987

Procedure

1973	1/73	Report of the Informal Committee on Reform of Dail Procedure
1975	M.75	Report of the Tribunal appointed by the Taoiseach on the 4th day of July, 1975 pursuant to Resolution passed on the 3rd day of July, 1975 by Dail Eireann and on the 4th day of July, 1975 by Seanad Eireann
1977	1/77	Report of the Committee on Procedure and Privileges on Amendment to Standing Order to Provide for Attendance of Minister of State Seanad Report
1979	1/79	Report of the Committee on Procedure and Privileges on Select and Special Committees
1979	2/79	Procedure for consideration by the Dail of the Estimates for Public Services.
		(Committee on Procedure and Privileges—Interim Report)
1980	2/80	Procedure for consideration by the Dail of the Estimates for Public Services
		(Committee on Procedure and Privileges—Report)
1982	1/82	Report of the Committee on Procedure and Privileges on procedures to enable the Seanad to invite distinguished persons to address it
1983	F168	Report of the Working Group on Cost over-Runs on Public Construction Contracts
1984	1/84	First Report of the Committee on Public Expenditure. Interim Report Recruitment by the Civil Service Commission and the Local Appointments Commission
1984	3/84	Committee on Public Expenditure. First Annual Progress Report
1984	4/84	Report of the Committee on Public Expenditure. Office of Public Works. 1. Project procedures used in the acquisition and fit out of premises. 2. Rental and lease terms in the period 1981–1983
1985	1/85	Report of the Committee on Procedure and Privileges on Amendment to Standing Order 69 to provide for the engagement of Consultants by the Committee
1986	F172	An Outline of Government Contracts Procedures
1987	7/87	25th Report of the Dail Committee on Public Expenditure. International Comparisons of Parliamentary Accountability for Public Expenditure

| 1988 | U119 | Report of the National Statistics Board. Strategy for Statistics 1988–1992 |
| 1991 | F/179 | Internal Audit Standards |

Parliament and the Departments

1977	M.77	Legislative Work of the 20th Dail, 1973–1977
1980	K124	Dail Eireann Constituency Commission Report 21st April, 1980
1981	M77/1	Legislative Work of the 21st Dail 1977–1981
1983	K124/1	Dail Constituency Commission. Report 29th July, 1983
1984	2/84	Report of the Committee on Public Expenditure. Proposal to establish a centralised State Agency for persons registering for Employment or Training
1985	2/85	Report of the Committee on Public Expenditure. Review of Department of the Public Service
1985	Y15	A New Institutional Structure for the Central Statistics Office
1986	F72/19	State Directory 1986
1987	1/87	17th Report of the Dail Committee on Public Expenditure. The Proposed Department of Defence/Army headquarters
1987	6/87	24th Report of the Dail Committee on Public Expenditure. The Industrial Development Authority. A view of certain aspects of of its public expenditure
1990	K/124/03	Dail Constituency Commission Report 1990
1990	R/147	Report Of The Commission On Remuneration And Conditions Of Service In The Defence Forces
1991	O/R 02/92	Committee of Public Accounts Special Report on Computer Security in Government Departments and Offices
1992	F/180	The Role of the Comptroller and Auditor General. A White Paper

Civil Service

1978	F100/1	Review Body on Higher Remuneration in the Public Sector. Reports to Minister for Finance and Minister for the Public Service in the period 13 July 1973 to 11 February 1977
1979	F100/2	Review Body on Higher Remuneration in the Public Sector
1982	F100/3	Review Body on Higher Remuneration in the Public Sector. Report No. 27 to the Minister for the Public Service on the levels of Remuneration appropriate to Higher Departmental and Professional Civil Service Posts, 27 November 1981
1985	F171	Serving the Country Better. A White Paper on the Public Service

1987	F100/4	Review Body on Higher Remuneration in the Public Sector. Report No. 30
1990	M/80	Subsistence Rates For Civil Servants In Ireland 1990
1992	M/82	Subsistence Rates for Civil Servants in Ireland, 1992

Local Government and Finance

1972	K105	Strengthening the Local Government Service (McKinsey)
1973	K.108	Local Finance and Taxation
1975	K.111	Powers Vested in Elected Members of Local Authorities
1975	R.127	Report of the Fire Service
1976	K.112	Explanatory Memorandum to the Local Government Planning and Development Act, 1976
1977	K.115	Working Party on Local Authority Superannuation-Interim Report
1980	K110/1	Local Elections, 1979 Election Results and Transfer of Votes and Election Statistics
1981	K 111/1	Guide to Local Government for Councillors
1982	K128	Explanatory memorandum to Local Government (Planning and Development) Bill, 1982
1985	K133	Dublin Electoral Area Boundaries Commission Report
1985	K134	County and County Borough Electoral Area Boundaries Commission Report
1985	K136	The Reform of Local Government. Policy Statement
1986	K110/2	Local Elections, 1985 Election Results and Transfer of Votes in respect of each County, and County Borough Council and Election Statistics relating to all local authorities
1987	K137	Public Library Service Review Group Report
1991	K/147	Local Government Reorganisation and Reform
1991	K/148	Local Government and the Elected Member
1992	K/159	Rate Support Grant Distribution in Ireland

International Relations

1972	F46/21	1. American Loan Counterpart Fund, 1969–70
1972	F46/22	2. American Grant Counterpart Special Account, 1970–71
1974	F.46/23	I. American Loan Counterpart Fund, 1971–72; II. American Grant Counterpart Special Account, 1971–72
1974	M.74	Northern Ireland-Agreed Communique issued following the Conference between the Irish and British Governments and the parties involved in the Northern Ireland Executive (designate) on 6th, 7th, 8th and 9th December, 1973
1977	F.46/25	(1) American Loan Counterpart Fund, 1973–74; (2) American Grant Counterpart Special Account, 1973–74

1977	F.46/26	(1) American Loan Counterpart Fund, 1st April 1974–31st December, 1974; (2) American Grant Counterpart Special Account—1st April 1974–31st December, 1974
1981	F46/27	American Loan Counterpart Fund 1st January, 1976–31st December, 1976
1982	F46/28	American Loan Counterpart Fund, 1st January, 1978–31st December, 1978
1983	F46/29	American Loan Counterpart Fund 1st January 1977–31st December, 1977
1984	F46/32	American Loan Counterpart Fund. 1st January, 1981–31st December, 1981
1983	PP65	New Ireland Forum—Issue No. 1 Public Session Monday 30th May 1983. Report of Proceedings
1984	PP65/1	The Cost of Violence arising from the Northern Ireland Crisis since 1969
1984	PP65/2	No. 2. Public Session, Wednesday 21 September, 1983
1984	PP65/3	No. 3. Public Session, Tuesday 4 October, 1983
1984	PP65/4	No. 4. Public Session, Wednesday 5 October, 1983
1984	PP65/5	No. 5. Public Session, Thursday 6 October,1983
1984	PP65/6	No. 6. Public Session, Tuesday 11 October, 1983
1984	PP65/7	No. 7. Public Session, Thursday 20 October, 1983
1984	PP65/8	No. 8. Public Session, Thursday 3 November, 1983
1984	PP65/9	No. 9. Public Session, Thursday 17 November, 1983
1984	PP65/10	No. 10. Public Session, Thursday 8 December, 1983
1984	PP65/11	No. 11. Public Session, Thursday 19 January, 1984
1984	PP65/12	No. 12. Public Session, Thursday 9 February, 1984
1984	PP65/13	No. 13. Public Session, Wednesday 2 May, 1984
1984	PP65/14	The Economic Consequences of the Division of Ireland since 1920
1984	PP65/15	A Comparative Description of the Economic Structure and Situation, North and South
1984	PP65/16	The Legal Systems, North and South
1984	PP65/17	Final Report
1984	PP65/18	The Macroeconomic Consequences of Integrated Economic Policy, Planning and Co-ordination in Ireland
1984	PP65/19	An Analysis of Agricultural Developments in the North and South of Ireland and of the Effects of Integrated Policy and Planning
1984	PP65/20	Opportunities for North/South Co-operation and Integration in Energy
1984	PP65/21	Integrated Policy and Planning for Transport in a New Ireland
1984	PP66	Houses of the Oireachtas. Joint Sitting. Address by Ronald Reagan, President of the United States of America. Monday, 4 June, 1984

1985	Y16	Anglo-Irish Agreement, 1985
1986	2/86	Second Report of the Joint Committee on Co-operation with Developing Countries. The Bilateral Aid programme
1986	H93	The American Commission on Irish Independence 1919. The Diary Correspondence and Report
1987	18/86	Fifth Report of the Joint Committee on Cooperation with Developing Countries Development Education
1989	Y/16/02	The Anglo-Irish Agreement. Review of The Working of The Conference
1990	X/64	Concluding Document on the Vienna Meeting 1986 of the participating states of the Conference on Security and Cooperation in Europe

State-Sponsored Bodies

1979	17/79	Second Report of the Joint Committee on State-Sponsored Bodies (British and Irish Steam Packet Company LTD.)
1979	R141	Report of Posts & Telegraphs Review Group
1980	4/80	Eighth Report of the Joint Committee on State-Sponsored Bodies (Bord Na Mona)
1980	11/80	Ninth Report of the Joint Committee on State-Sponsored Bodies (Aer Rianta, Teoranta)
1980	12/80	Sixth Report of the Joint Committee on State-Sponsored Bodies (Aer Rianta, Teoranta)
1980	13/80	Tenth Report of the Joint Committee on State-Sponsored Bodies (The Agricultural Credit Corporation, Limited)
1980	15/80	Seventh Report of the Joint Committee on State-Sponsored Bodies (Arramara Teoranta)
1980	19/80	Eleventh Report of the Joint Committee on State-Sponsored Bodies (Industrial Credit Company, Limited)
1981	1/81	Twelfth Report of the Joint Committee on State-Sponsored Bodies (National Building Agency Limited)
1981	2/81	Thirteenth Report of the Joint Committee on State-Sponsored Bodies (Comhlucht Siuicre Eireann, Teoranta)
1981	4/81	Fourteenth Report of the Joint Committee on State-Sponsored Bodies (Aer Lingus, Teoranta and Aerlinte Eireann, Teoranta)
1981	5/81	Fifteenth Report of the Joint Committee on State-Sponsored Bodies (Irish Shipping Limited)
1981	10/81	Sixteenth Report of the Joint Committee on State-Sponsored Bodies (Nitrigin Eireann Teoranta)
1981	11/81	Eighteenth Report of the Joint Committee on State-Sponsored Bodies (Radio Telefis Eireann)
1981	12/81	Seventeenth Report of the Joint Committee on State-Sponsored Bodies (Foir Teoranta)

1981	13/81	3rd Report of the Joint Committee on State-Sponsored Bodies (Min Their (1959) Teo.)
1981	15/81	Fourth Report of the Joint Committee on State-Sponsored Bodies (Coras Iompair Eireann)
1983	6/82	Joint Committee on State-Sponsored Bodies—Special Report —Udaras na Gaeltachta
1984	5/84	Joint Committee on Commercial State-Sponsored Bodies. First Report Ostlanna Iompair Eireann Teoranta
1985	5/85	Joint Committee on Commercial State-Sponsored Bodies. Second Report. Irish Shipping Limited
1986	3/86	Joint Committee on Commercial State-Sponsored Bodies. Third Report Bord Gais Eireann
1986	8/86	Joint Committee on Commercial State-Sponsored Bodies. Fourth Report Udaras na Gaeltachta
1986	17/86	Joint Committee on Commercial State-Sponsored Bodies. Fifth Report. Analysis of financial position of Commercial State-Sponsored Bodies based on latest published accounts
1987	21/86	Joint Committee on Commercial State-Sponsored Bodies. Sixth Report. Electricity Supply Board
1987	3/87	Joint Committee on Commercial State-Sponsored Bodies. Seventh Report. Bord Telecom Eireann
1988	1/88	Joint Committee on Commercial State-Sponsored Bodies. First Report. Irish Life Assurance plc
1988	4/88	Fifth Joint Committee on Commercial State-Sponsored Bodies. Second Report. An Post
1988	5/88	Fifth Joint Committee on Commercial State-Sponsored Bodies. Third Report. B & I Line plc
1988	10/88	Fifth Joint Committee on Commercial State-Sponsored Bodies. Fourth Report. Irish Steel Limited
1989	O/R/89/01	Fifth Joint Committee on Commercial State-Sponsored Bodies. Aer Lingus PLC and Aerlinte Eireann PLC
1990	O/R/90/01	Sixth Joint Committee on Commercial State-Sponsored Bodies. First Report—The Irish National Stud Company Limited
1990	O/R/90/02	Sixth Joint Committee on Commercial State-Sponsored Bodies. Second Report. Irish National Petroleum Corporation Limited
1990	O/R/90/03	Sixth Joint Committee on Commercial State-Sponsored Bodies. Third Report. An Post-An Post National Lottery Company
1992	O/R/ 04/91	Sixth Joint Committee on Commercial State-Sponsored Bodies. Fourth Report. Bord Na Mona
1992	O/R/06/92	Sixth Joint Committee on Commercial State-Sponsored Bodies. 5th Report. Bord Na gCon

1992	P/P/70/01	Joint Committee on Commercial State-Sponsored Bodies. Minutes of Evidence. Bord Na gCon
1992	P/P/70/02	Joint Committee On Commercial State-Sponsored Bodies. An Post—An Post National Lottery Company
1992	P/P/70/04	Joint Committee on Commercial State-Sponsored Bodies. Minutes of Evidence. Aer Rianta
1992	O/R 27/92	Sixth Joint Committee on Commercial State-Sponsored Bodies Seventh Report. Aer Rianta CPT
1992	O/R 28/92	Joint Committee on Commercial State-Sponsored Bodies. Minutes of Evidence. The Irish National Stud Company Limited

POLITICAL AND ECONOMIC RELATIONS WITH THE EUROPEAN COMMUNITY

Oireachtas Reports of the Joint Committees on the
Secondary Legislation of the European Communities.

1973	1/73	First Report, Vol I, August, 1973
	2/73	Second Report, Vol I, September, 1973
	3/73	Vol I, No. 3, October, 1973
	4/73	Vol I, No. 4, October, 1973
	5/73	Vol I, No. 5, October, 1973
	6/73	Vol I, No. 6, November, 1973
1974	4/74	First
	5/74	Second
	6/74	Third
1975	4/75	Fourth
	5/75	Fifth (Budgetary Powers EC Parliament)
	6/75	Sixth (Fertilizer and pigmeat)
	7/75	Seventh (Direct Elections EC Parliament)
	7A/75	Eighth (Statutory Instruments, 1972 Act)
	8/75	Ninth (Equal treatment, men and women)
	10/75	Tenth (Disadvantaged areas)
	11/75	Eleventh (EC Directories)
	12/75	Twelfth (Statutory Instruments, 1972 Act)
	13/75	Thirteenth (Credit institutions)
	14/75	Fourteenth (EC Monetary Cooperation Fund)
	15/75	Fifteenth (Pollutions of seawater)
1976	3/76	Sixteenth (Tariff Preference Scheme)
	2/76	Seventeenth (Sheepmeat)
	6/76	Eighteenth (Road Worthiness Test)
	4/76	Nineteenth (Forestry measures)

1976	15/76	Twentieth (Poultry meat)
	7/76	Twenty-first (Miscellaneous regulations)
	8/76	Twenty-second (Statutory Instruments, 1972 Act)
	20/76	Twenty-third (Agricultural prices)
	23/76	Twenty-fourth (Young farmer's aid)
	21/76	Twenty-fifth (Animal transport)
	28/76	Twenty-sixth (Company taxation)
	24/76	Twenty-seventh (Chemicals, customs)
	25/76	Twenty-eighth (Water content, fowl)
	30/76	Twenty-ninth (Transport, bus and coach)
	32/76	Thirtieth (Implementation)
	34/76	Thirty-first (Potato market)
	33/76	Thirty-second (Beekeeper's aid)
	36/76	Thirty-third (Driver's Licenses)
	37/76	Thirty-fourth (Measurements)
	38/76	Thirty-fifth (Right to open business)
	39/76	Thirty-sixth (Tax exemptions)
	42/76	Thirty-seventh (Fishing industry)
	35/76	Thirty-eighth (Protection of farm animals)
	43/76	Thirty-ninth (Road transport)
	40/76	Fortieth (Statutory Instruments, 1972 Act)
	41/76	Forty-first (Taxes on tobacco)
	44/76	Forty-second (Public companies)
1977	1/77	Forty-third (Tariffs)
	2/77	Forty-fourth (Reform of agriculture)
	3/77	Forty-fifth (Milk)
	4/77	Forty-sixth (Packaging)
	5/77	Forty-seventh (Company Law)
	6/77	Forty-eighth (Securities)
	7/77	Forty-ninth (Statutory Instruments)
	9/77	Fiftieth (Urban air pollution)
	8/77	Fifty-first (Mutual assistance direct taxation)
	12/77	Fifty-second (Evergreen Export Bank)
	11/77	Fifty-third (Product liability)
	14/77	Fifty-fourth (Transferable securities)
	13/77	Fifty-fifth (Joint Committees)
	16/77	Fifty-sixth (Equal treatment social security)
	15/77	Fifty-seventh (Penalties)
	10/77	Fifty-eighth (Fresh poultry meat)
	17/77	Fifty-ninth (Toxic wastes)
1978	3/78	First (Mergers)
	1/78	Second (Dental Surgeons)
	4/78	Third (Life Assurance)
	5/78	Fourth (Beef and veal markets)

1978	6/78	Fifth (Agricultural structures)
	13/78	Sixth (Common Agricultural Policy)
	7/78	Seventh (Shipbuilding)
	8/78	Eighth (Doorstep sales)
	9/78	Ninth (Homestudy courses)
	2/78	Tenth (Youth employment)
	10/78	Eleventh (Group accounts)
	11/78	Twelfth (Public companies)
	14/78	Thirteenth (Sheep meat)
	15/78	Fourteenth (Economic and Monetary Union)
	12/78	Fifteenth (Petroleum stocks)
	16/78	Sixteenth (Misleading advertising)
	17/78	Seventeenth (Social insurance for self employed)
	18/78	Eighteenth (Health and safety at work)
	19/78	Nineteenth (Pollution, air and water)
	20/78	Twentieth (Statutory instruments)
1979	5/79	Twenty-first (Cultural sector)
	7/79	Twenty-second (VAT on art)
	21/79	Twenty-third (Teaching of languages)
	3/79	Twenty-fourth (Study of EC)
	8/79	Twenty-fifth (Veterinary Medicine products)
	4/79	Twenty-sixth (Veterinary Medicine practice)
	1/79	Twenty-seventh (Agricultural research)
	2/79	Twenty-eighth (Control of concentrations)
	6/79	Twenty-ninth (Statutory Instruments)
	9/79	Thirtieth (Employee protection from insolvent employer)
	12/79	Thirty-first (Statutory audits)
	13/79	Thirty-second (Milk sector)
	10/79	Thirty-third (Tariffs)
	15/79	Thirty-fourth (Public transport)
	11/79	Thirty-fifth (Illegal migration)
	14/79	Thirty-sixth (Noise and water pollution)
	16/79	Thirty-seventh (Energy)
	22/79	Thirty-eighth (Marine oil pollution)
	20/79	Thirty-ninth (Customs)
	23/79	Fortieth (Recycling waste)
	21/79	Forty-first (Forestry policy)
	18/79	Forty-second (Water content, fowl)
	24/79	Forty-third (Company tax harmonization)
	19/79	Forty-fourth (State instruments)
	30/79	Forty-fifth (Agricultural structures)
	25/79	Forty-sixth (Swine fever)
	31/79	Forty-seventh (Community Budget)
	34/79	Forty-eighth (Energy labels on products)

1979	26/79	Fiftieth (Statutory instruments)
	27/79	Fifty-first (EC enlargement)
	28/79	Fifty-second (Quotas)
	29/79	Fifty-third (Ionizing radiation)
	33/79	Fifty-fourth (Construction products)
	32/79	Fifty-fifth (Weights of vehicles)
	35/79	Fifty-sixth (Tower cranes)
1980	3/80	Forty-ninth (Information on traded companies)
	2/80	Fifty-seventh (AETR agreement)
	1/80	Fifty-eighth (Financing Community Budget)
	14/80	Fifty-ninth (Industrial restructuring)
	5/80	Sixtieth (R & D, Textiles and Clothing)
	7/80	Sixty-first (Tariffs)
	9/80	Sixty-second (Customs declarations)
	16/80	Sixty-third (Exchange of young workers)
	6/80	Sixty-fourth (Units of measurement)
	8/80	Sixty-fifth (Quality of food)
	10/80	Sixty-sixth (Statutory Instruments)
	20/80	Sixty-seventh (Joint Committee)
	21/80	Sixty-eighth (Insurance contracts)
	22/80	Sixty-ninth (Agricultural Markets)
	17/80	Seventieth (Work sharing)
	18/80	Seventy-third (Waste regulations)
	23/80	Seventy-fourth (Combating poverty)
1981	3/81	Seventy-fifth (Statutory Instruments)
	6/81	Seventy-first (Discharge of Mercury)
	7/81	Seventy-seventh (Common Fisheries Policy)
	8/81	Seventy-ninth (Consumer credit)
1982	5/82	Seventy-sixth (Community aid for infrastructure in Ireland)
	1/82	Ninetieth (Liability, defective products)
	3/82	Ninety-first (Inter Regional air services)
	2/82	Ninety-second (Textile Labelling)
	4/82	Ninety-third (Labour Market Policy)
	2/85	Fourth Joint Committee(Equality of opportunity)
	4/85	Fourth Joint Committee (Report #14) (European Union)
	15/86	Fourth Joint Committee (Report #33) (Aquaculture)
1992	O/R 01/92	Sixth Joint Committee Report #11 (Common Fisheries Policy)
	O/R 04/92	Sixth Joint Committee Report #12
	O/R 17/92	Sixth Joint Committee Report #13 (Agriculture)
	O/R 24/92	European Communities Report #14 (Excise taxes)
1972	F95	The Accession of Ireland to the European Communities
1972	F96	The Accession of Ireland to the European Communities Supplement to the White Paper

1972	X40	Treaty establishing the European Economic Community, Rome, 25th March, 1957
1972	X41	Treaty concerning the Accession of the Kingdom of Denmark, Ireland, the Kingdom of Norway and the United Kingdom to the European Economic Community and the European Atomic Energy Community and Related Instruments,
1973	I.136	E.E.C. Policy on Restrictive Trade Practices
1977	R.137	European Assembly Constituency Commission Report, 4th October, 1977
1978	F159	The European Monetary System
1978	I 160	Restrictive Practices Commission. EEC Policy on Competition —A Guide for Businessmen
1989	Y/24	Europen–1992 and the Construction Sector
1990	X/65	Irish Presidency of the European Communities January– June 1990
1990	Y/24/01	Europen–1992 and the Metal and Mechanical Engineering Sector
1990	Y/24/02	Europen–1992 and the Food and Drink Industry
1990	Y/24/03	Europen–1992 and the Textile Clothing and Footwear Sector
1990	Y/24/04	Europen–1992 and the Electronic, Electrical and Instrument Engineering Sectors
1990	Y/24/05	Europen–1992 and the Pharmaceutical, Healthcare and Chemicals Sector
1990	Y/24/06	Europen–1992 and the Tourism Sector
1990	Y/24/07	Europen–1992 and the Transport Sector
1990	Y/24/08	Europen–1992 and the Financial Services Sector
1992	I/211	Fair Trade Commission. EEC Policy on Competition. A guide for Irish Business, 4th Edition
1992	X/67	White Paper Treaty On European Union
1992	X/68	Ireland in Europe. A Shared Challenge. Economic Co-operation On The Island of Ireland In An Integrated Europe

NATIONAL FINANCE

1972	F102	Company Taxation in Ireland
1974	F.108	Company Taxation in Ireland Proposals for Corporation Tax
1976	F.138	An Outline of Irish Financial Procedures
1978	1/78	Report of the Special Committee on the Value-Added Tax (Amendment) Bill, 1977
1980	U108	Redistributive Effects of State Taxes and Benefits on Household Incomes in 1973
1981	Y11	A Better Way to Plan the Nation's Finances
1982	F167	First Report of the Commission on Taxation (Direct Taxation) July 1982

1984	F167/1	Second Report of the Commission on Taxation (Direct Taxation) March, 1984
1984	F167/2	Third Report of the Commission on Taxation (Indirect Taxation) June 1984
1985	3/85	Report of the Committee on Public Expenditure. Service of Public Debt
1985	4/85	Report of the Committee on Public Expenditure. Control of Capital Projects
1985	F167/3	Fourth Report of the Commission on Taxation. Special Taxation
1985	F167/4	Fifth Report of the Commission on Taxation (including index to the five reports). Tax Administration, October 1985
1986	7/86	20th Report of the Dail Committee on Public Expenditure. A schedule of recommendations arising from the work of the Committee relating to immediately implementable public sector savings and management improvement
1987	3/87	26th Report of the Dail Committee on Public Expenditure. Annual Progress Report, 1986
1987	F174	Framework for 1987 Budget
1992	F/181	Government Proposals for Legislation to be included in a Second Finance Bill

MONEY AND MONETARY POLICY

| 1972 | F97 | Irish Decimal Currency Board Final Report, 1970–71 |

AGRICULTURE, FOOD, AND FORESTRY

General Policy

1974	A.71	Farm Records and Accounts
1975	A.72	A National Agricultural Advisory Education and Research Authority-White paper
1977	R.136	Inter-Departmental Committee on Land Structure Reform—Interim Report, May, 1977
1978	R138	Inter-Departmental Committee on Land Structure Reform Final Report
1980	A75	Land Policy
1984	A80	Four-Year Plan for Agriculture Report of the Working Group
1986	A84	Report of AFT/ACOT Review Group presented to the Minister for Agriculture on 13th March 1986
1991	A/87	Agriculture and Food Policy Review
1992	A/88	Pesticide Residues in Food–1991

Particular Products

1973	I.133/6	National Prices Commission—Occasional Paper No. 7. The Marketing of Fruit and Vegetables. March, 1973
1975	I.140	Meat Prices Advisory Body—Report of Enquiry into the Domestic Meat Trade
1979	A74	Report of Study Group on Milk Recording
1979	I 133/29	National Prices Commission Occasional Paper No. 30. The Dublin Fruit and Vegetable Wholesale Market
1982	A77	Tomato Production in Ireland
1982	A78	Processed Vegetable Industry in Ireland
1984	A82	Sheep—Production, Disease and Marketing
1987	5/87	The 22nd Report of the Dail Committee on Public Expenditure. Review of the Public Expenditure Programme for the Eradication of Bovine Tuberculosis
1989	A/86	Milk Quota Review Group. Report to the Minister for Agriculture and Food, Mr. Michael O'Kennedy T.D.

Forestry and Fisheries

1972	L62	Forest Research Review, 1964–70
1984	G25	The Case for Forestry (1980, revised 1983)
1985	G27	Review Group on the Forestry
1986	5/86	Dail Committee on Public Expenditure, 14th Report. State Support and Services to the Fishing Industry
1987	9/87	21st Report of the Dail Committee on Public Expenditure. A Review of State Expenditure on The Forest and Wildlife Service
1989	G/36	Fishing Vessel Safety
1991	L/57/33	Ireland Forestry Operational Programme 1989–1993

ECONOMIC POLICY: DEVELOPMENT, PLANNING AND TRADE

Resources and Industries

1972	I.131/7	Committee on Industrial Progress. Report on Footwear Industry
1972	I.131/8	Committee on Industrial Progress. Report on the Woollen and Worsted Industry
1972	I.131/9	Committee on Industrial Progress. Report on Shirtmaking Industry
1973	I.131/10	C.O.I.P. Report on Furniture Industry

1973	I.135	Committee of Inquiry into the Insurance Industry. Interim Report on Motor Insurance
1973	I.137	Committee on Industrial Progress-General Report
1974	K.109	Report of the Committee on the Price of Building Land
1976	I.145	The Irish Agricultural Engineering Industry (James Kenny)
1976	R.132	Committee of Inquiry into the Insurance Industry. Final Report
1976	I.153	Report of Enquiry into the Fertiliser Industry
1978	I 133/23	National Prices Commission Occasional Papers No. 24. Study of Taxi and Hackney Services
1978	I 133/25	National Prices Commission Occasional Paper No. 26. Motor Vehicle Assembly Study
1978	I 133/28	National Prices Commission Occasional Paper No. 28. The Irish Market for White Electrical Goods
1978	Y2	The Irish Services Sector. A Study of Productive Efficiency. D.J. Cogan
1979	I 167	Interim Report of the Inter-Departmental Committee appointed by the Minister for Industry, Commerce and Energy to consider possible uses of Bord na Mona cutaway bogs
1980	I 169	Report on Motor Insurance Rating, Loading and Claims Statistics in respect of the year 1978
1981	F166	Report of the Committee on Costs and Competitiveness
1982	I169/1	Report on Motor Insurance Rating, Loading and Claims Statistics in respect of the year 1979
1983	I177	Report of Enquiry into the Cost and Methods of Providing Motor Insurance, 1982
1984	2/84	First Report of the Joint Committee on Small Businesses. Manufacturing Industry
1984	7/84	Second Report of the Joint Committee on Small Businesses. Retail and Distribution
1984	U 113	Survey of the Structure and Distribution of Earnings in Industry. Distribution, Credit and Insurance. October 1979
1985	6/85	Third Report of the Joint Committee on Small Businesses, Tourism, Catering and Leisure
1985	9/85	Report of the Joint Committee on Building Land
1986	1/86	Fourth Report of the Joint Committee on Small Businesses Construction
1986	6/86	Fifth Report of the Joint Committee on Small Businesses. The insurance problems of small businesses
1986	13/86	Sixth Report of the Joint Committee on Small Businesses. The development and management of small business co-operatives
1986	A85	Report of the Commission of Inquiry into the thoroughbred Horse Breeding Industry

1986	I184	Report of the Courseware Committee
1987	I189	Review of Industrial Performance 1986
1987	R146	Report of the Task Force on Multi-Storey Buildings
1989	K/142	Construction Industry in Ireland. Review of 1988. Outlook for 1989
1989	W/13	Peatlands. Wastelands or Heritage?
1990	K/143	Construction Industry in Ireland. Review Of 1989, Outlook For 1990

Technology, Research and Development, Science

1972	F101	Science Policy Formulation and Resource Allocation
1972	F85/1	National Science Council Research and Development in Ireland, 1969
1973	F.103	National Science Council—Progress Report, 1969–71
1973	F.104	Ireland—Background Report on Science and Technology
1973	F.104/1	National Science Council—Studies in Irish Science Policy
1973	F.104/2	Science, Technology and Industry in Ireland. C. Cooper and N. Whelan
1974	F.105	Research and Development in Ireland, 1971
1974	F.106	Fellowships and Scholarships available to Irish Scientists and Technologists. D. Murphy and M. Fitzgerald
1976	I.146	Technology Transfer
1976	I.147	Innovation in Ireland-Case Studies (Dermot P. O'Doherty)
1976	I.150	National Science Council-Research and Development in Ireland, 1974 by Diarmuid Murphy and Liam O Cuanaigh
1976	I.151	Technological Supports for the Food Industry, W. K. Downey and M. J. Brennan
1977	I.157	National Science Council-Research Planning and Innovation
1978	Y3	National Science Council. Scientific and Technical Information in Ireland: Financial Resources Devoted to S.T.I.D. in Ireland, 1975
1978	Y4	Research and Development in Ireland 1975 by Conor Maguire and Diarmuid Murphy
1978	Y6	National Science Council. Scientific and Technical Information in Ireland: The findings of the National Documentation Use Study. Vol. 1 by Barre Carroll and Norman Wood
1978	Y6/1	National Science Council. Scientific and Technical Information in Ireland: The Findings of the National Documentation Use Study. Vol. 2 by Barre Carroll and Norman Wood
1987	2/87	Seventh Report of the Joint Committee on Small Businesses. New Technology and the Small Business

Consumer Interests, Prices, Statistical Practices

1972	I.133	National Prices Commission Occasional Paper, No. 1. Consumer Councils in Public Enterprise
1972	I.133/1	National Prices Commission Occasional Paper, No. 2. Report on New House Prices
1973	I.133/2	National Prices Commission Occasional Paper, No. 3. The Price of Drink. November, 1972
1973	I.133/3	National Prices Commission Occasional Paper, No. 4. C.I.E. Rates and Fares. December, 1972
1973	I.133/4	National Prices Commission Occasional Paper, No. 5. Consumer Protection, A Role for Local Government
1973	I.133/5	National Prices Commission Occasional Paper, No. 6. Consumer Councils in Private Enterprises. April, 1973
1973	I.133/9	National Prices Commission Occasional Paper, No. 10. The Pricing Policy of Coras Iompair Eireann. July, 1973
1974	I.133/10	National Prices Commission Occasional Paper, No. 11. The Animal Feedstuffs Industry in Ireland, December, 1973
1974	I.133/11	National Prices Commission Occasional Paper, No. 12. Retail Petrol Margins, February, 1974
1974	I.133/12	National Prices Commission Occasional Paper, No. 13. Charges for Pathology Services, February, 1974
1974	I.133/13	National Prices Commission Occasional Paper, No. 14. Building Societies in Ireland, February, 1974
1974	I.133/14	National Prices Commission Occasional Paper, No. 15. A Report on The Services Provided by Auctioneers, April, 1974. R. Harrington
1974	I.133/15	National Prices Commission Occasional Paper, No. 16. The Irish Flour Industry, May, 1974
1975	I.141	National Consumer Advisory Council, Submissions to the Minister for Industry and Commerce on proposals for legislation to assure the consumers' interests
1977	I.133/20	National Prices Commission Occasional Paper, No. 21. Department of Posts and Telegraphs December 1976
1978	I 164	Report of Consumer Education Committee
1979	U107	Report of the Interdepartmental Study Group on Unemployment Statistics

Tourism

1985	I183	White Paper on Tourism Policy
1987	2/87	23rd Report of the Dáil Committee on Public Expenditure on Tourism
1987	T35	Improving the Performance of Irish Tourism. Summary

| 1987 | T36 | Improving the Performance of Irish Tourism. Main Report |
| 1992 | T/39 | Report of the Tourism Task Force to the Minister for Tourism, Transport and Communications |

Competition and Fair Trade

1972	I.101/42	Fair Trade Commission. Report of Enquiry into the conditions which obtain in regard to the supply and distribution of Motor Spirit
1972	I.101/43	Fair Trade Commission. Report of Enquiry into the conditions which obtain in regard to the supply and distribution of Grocery Goods for human consumption
1973	I.134	Restrictive Practices Commission. Report of Enquiry into Supply and Distribution of Iron and Steel Scrap
1975	R.129	Coal Prices Advisory Body. Report of Enquiry into the Coal Trade
1975	R.130	Motor Premiums Advisory Committee. Report on Applications for Increases in Motor Insurance Premiums
1976	I.154	Restrictive Practices Commission. Report of Study of Roadside and Street Trading and Sales from Temporary Retail Outlets
1977	I.156	Restrictive Practices Commission. Report of Study of Competition in the Licensed Drink Trade
1978	I 162	Restrictive Practices Commission. Report of Studies into Industrial Concentration and Mergers in Ireland
1976	I.148	Restrictive Practices Commission. Report of Special Review by Means of Public Enquiry of the Operation of Article 2 and 3 of the Restrictive Practices (Groceries) Order, 1973, as amended by the Restrictive Practices (Groceries) (Amendment) Order, 1973
1981	I 173	Report of Enquiry into the Retail Sale of Grocery Goods below cost
1981	I 174	Motor Spirit Enquiry Report, 1980
1985	I181	Restrictive Practices Commission. Report of Inquiry into the effects on competition of the restrictions on Conveyancing and the restrictions on Advertising by Solicitors, 1982
1985	I182	Restrictive Practices Commission. Report of Enquiry into the provision of Tour Operator and Travel Agency Services insofar as they are affected by the activities of Associations in the Travel Trade
1986	I186	Restrictive Practices Commission. Report of Enquiry into the Policies of Building Societies in regard to Insurance Related to Mortgaged Properties and Valuation Reports on Properties 1985

1986	I187	Restrictive Practices Commission. Report of Study into Cable Television Systems in the Greater Dublin Area, 1986
1988	I194	Restrictive Practices Commission. Report on alleged Differences in Retail Grocery Prices between the Republic of Ireland and the United Kingdom (including particularly Northern Ireland) 1987
1988	I196	Restrictive Practices Commission. Report of Study into concerted Fixing of Fees and Restrictions on Advertising in the Engineering Profession 1987
1989	I/199	Public Enquiry into The Supply and Distribution of Motor Fuels by the Fair Trade Commission
1990	I/201	Fair Trade Commission Report of Study Into Restrictive Practices in the Legal Profession
1991	I/204	Fair Trade Commission Study of Competition Law
1991	I/205	Fair Trade Commission Report of Enquiry Into The Supply and Distribution of Motor Fuels
1991	I/207	Fair Trade Commission Report of the Review of the Restrictive Practices (Groceries) Order, 1987

Economic Development

1974	F.112	A National Partnership
1976	F.136	Economic and Social Development 1976–1980
1978	Y1	National Development 1977–1980
1978	Y5	Development for Full Employment
1979	Y7	Programme for National Development 1978–1981 (White Paper)
1980	Y8	Investment and National Development 1979–1983
1981	Y10	Investment Plan 1981
1982	Y12	The Way Forward. National Economic Plan 1983–1987
1984	I 179	Industrial Policy (White Paper)
1984	Y 13	Building on Reality 1985–1987
1984	Y 13/1	Building on Reality 1985–1987. A Summary
1986	3/86	Report of the Committee on Public Expenditure. Review of Shannon Free Airport Development Company Limited
1987	Y19	Programme for National Recovery
1989	Y/22	National Development Plan 1989–1993
1989	Y/23	National Development Plan 1989–1993
1990	I/200/01	Programme for Industrial Development Summary
1991	I/189/1	Review of Industrial Performance 1990
1991	Y/25	Programme for Economic and Social Progress
1992	I/208	A Time For Change: Industrial Policy for the 1990s Report of The Industrial Policy Review Group

1992   I/208/01   A Time for Change: Industrial Policy For the 1990s. Reform of The Irish Taxation System From An Industrial Point of View

1992   I/208/02   A Time For Change: Industrial Policy for the 1990s. The Food Industry

1992   I/208/03   A Time for Change: Industrial Policy for the 1990s. Energy For Industry—A Policy Review

1992   I/208/04   A Time For Change: Industrial Policy for the 1990s. Industrial Promotion Agencies

1992   I/208/05   A Time For Change: Industrial Policy for the 1990s. The Medium Term Development of Indigenous Industry: The Role of The Financial Sector

1992   I/208/06   A Time For Change: Industrial Policy for the 1990s. Study On External Macroeconomic Issues

1992   I/208/07   A Time For Change: Industrial Policy for the 1990s. Economic Policy and Growth: The Context For Irish Industry

1992   I/208/08   A Time For Change: Industrial Policy for the 1990s. The Impact of Communications On Industry and Industrial Development

1992   I/208/09   A Time For Change: Industrial Policy for the 1990s. Privatisation

1992   I/208/10   A Time For Change: Industrial Policy for the 1990s. The Organisational Arrangements For The Formulation and Implementation of Industrial Policy in Ireland

1992   I/208/11   A Time For Change: Industrial Policy for the 1990s. The Impact of the Industrial Development Agencies

1992   I/208/12   A Time For Change: Industrial Policy for the 1990s. The Causes of Failure In Industrial Projects in Ireland & Suggestions for Action

1992   I/208/13   A Time For Change: Industrial Policy for the 1990s. A Comparative Study of Small Economies

1992   I/208/14   A Time For Change: Industrial Policy for the 1990s. Employee Participation

1992   I/208/15   A Time for Change: Industrial Policy for the 1990s. The Impact of Planning, Licensing and Environmental Issues on Industrial Development

1992   I/208/16   A Time For Change: Industrial Policy for the 1990s. Submission on Industrial Policy

1992   I/208/17   A Time For Change: Industrial Policy for the 1990s. Industrial Training in Ireland

TRANSPORTATION, ENERGY AND THE ENVIRONMENT

1974	R.124	Restructuring the Department of Transport and Power. The Separation of Policy and Execution

Energy and Water

1972	R115	Report by the E.S.B. Investigation Committee (Fletcher)
1975	F.128	Solar Energy for Ireland (Eamon Lalor)
1976	T.10	Energy Conservation in Ireland, 1975–1985
1977	I.159	Analysis of the Impact of Heat Pump Technology on the Irish Energy System to the year 2000—John Brady
1978	I 163	Energy—Ireland. Discussion Document on some Current Energy Problems and Options
1978	W7	River Maigue Drainage Scheme.Cost Benefit Analysis
1979	K122	Technical Committee on Effluent and Water Quality Standards. Memorandum No. 1. Water Quality Guidelines
1985	I180	Report of the Inquiry into Electricity Prices
1989	I/197	Electromagnetic Fields from High Voltage Transmission Lines. A Report to Mr Michael Smith, T.D., Minister for Energy
1990	K/146	Ireland Operational Programme: Water, Sanitary And Other Local Services 1989–1993

The Environment

1973	R.116	Report on Water Pollution
1975	T.6	The Climate of Ireland (P. K. Rohan)
1976	I.144	National Inventory of Research and Development in Environmental Pollution. W. K. Downey, A. J. O'Sullivan, S. E. Denham
1977	I.155	National Science Council.Water Pollution in Ireland P. F. Toner and A. J. O'Sullivan
1978	I 161	National Science Council Lake Pollution Eutrophication Control
1978	K117	Inter-Departmental Environment Committee Report on Pollution Control
1979	K121	Towards an Environment Policy
1980	T17	Report on the Disaster at Whiddy Island, Bantry, Co. Cork on 8th January, 1979
1980	K125	Litter and the Environment
1982	K125/1	A Policy for the Environment
1987	T6A	The Climate of Ireland. Second Edition
1987	T33	The Irish Meteorological Service. The First Fifty years 1936–1986
1991	K/153	Climate Change Studies on the Implications for Ireland

Transport

1979	K119	Road Development Plan for the 1980s
1980	R142	Report of the Transport Consultative Commission on Passenger Transport Services in the Dublin Area
1981	T18	The Transport Challenge: A report for the Minister for Transport by McKinsey International Inc
1981	R142/1	Report of the Transport Consultative Commission on Road Freight Haulage
1985	K132	Policy and Planning Framework for Roads. January 1985
1985	T32	Transport Policy. A Green Paper
1987	4/87	16th Report of the Dail Committee on Public Expenditure. Review of procedures relating to road openings by utilities
1988	G31	Dun Laoghaire Harbour. Report of the Planning Review Group
1989	G/35	Certificates of Competency in the Merchant Marine
1989	K/140	Operational Programme. Road Development 1989–1993
1989	T/38	Memorandum of Understanding between the Aeronautical Authorities of Ireland and of the United Kingdom
1990	K/144	Operational Programme On Peripherality Roads and Other Transport Infrastructure 1989–1993 [Main Report]
1990	K/145	Operational Programme On Peripherality Roads and Other Transport Infrastructure 1989–1993 [Summary]
1991	G/39	Report of Review Group on Air/Sea Rescue Services
1992	K/155/06	Dublin Transportation Study Phase 1 Final Report
1992	K/160	Inter-Departmental Report on Taxis and Hackneys

STATUS OF WOMEN

1973	R.117	Commission on the Status of Women. Report to the Minister for Finance, December, 1972
1977	R.135	Progress Report on the implementation of the Recommendations in the Report of the Commission on the Status of Women
1979	R135/1	Second Progress Report on the implementation of the Recommendations in the Report of the Commission on the Status of Women
1984	6/84	First Report of the Joint Committee on Women's Rights. Interim Report. Education
1985	3/85	Report of the Joint Committee on Marriage Breakdown
1985	Y14	Irish Women: Agenda for Practical Action
1986	7/86	Third Report of the Joint Committee on Women's Rights. Portrayal of women in the media

1987	1/87	Fourth Report of the Joint Committee on Women's Rights. Sexual Violence
1987	R145	Report on United Nations Convention on The Elimination of all Forms of Discrimination against Women
1988	3/88	First Report of the Second Joint Committee on Women's Rights
1988	6/88	Second Report of the Second Joint Committee on Women's Rights
1988	7/88	Third Report of the Second Joint Committee on Women's Rights
1989	Y/21	The Development of Equal Opportunities, March 1987– September 1988: Coordinated Report
1991	O/R/91/02	First Report of the Third Joint Committee on Women's Rights, Motherhood, Work and Equal Opportunity. A Case Study of Irish Civil Servants
1992	O/R 03/92	Second Report of the Third Joint Committee on Women's Rights. Gender Equality in Education in the Republic of Ireland. (1984–1991)
1992	J/121	Marital Breakdown A Review and Proposed Changes. (White Paper)
1992	Y/26	The Development of Equal Opportunities. Second Coordinated Report. October 1988–February 1992
1993	Y/29	Second Commission on the Status of Women. Report to Government January 1993

LABOUR

Employment, Labour Supply and Training

1975	R.125	Training and Employing the Handicapped
1980	E86	Development of Youth Work Services in Ireland
1983	V42	Working Party on Child Care Facilities for Working Parents
1984	V 44	National Youth Policy Committee. Final Report
1985	U.114	Population and Labor Force Projections, 1986–1991
1986	V45	'In Partnership with Youth' . . . The National Youth Policy
1986	V46	Manpower Policy White Paper
1988	U.114/1	Population and Labor Force Projections, 1991–2021
1989	V/095	Managers for Ireland. The Case for the Development of Irish Managers. Report and Recommendations of the Advisory Committee on Management Training
1992	O/R 08/92	Joint Committee on Employment. First Report

Trade Unions, Industrial Relations, Working Conditions

1980	Y9	Worker Participation. A Discussion Paper
1981	V41	Report of the Commission of Enquiry on Industrial Relations
1984	V 43	Report of the Commission of Inquiry on Safety, Health and Welfare at Work
1986	V47	Employers' Perceptions of the effect of Labour Legislation
1986	V48	Report of the Advisory Committee on Worker Participation
1988	V49	A Study of Unofficial Strikes in Ireland
1988	Y20	Workers In Union. National Archives Documents and Commentaries on the History of Irish Labour. Edited by Fergus A D'Arcy and Ken Hannigan

SOCIAL SERVICE AND SECURITY

1974	N.2	Guide to the Social Services, 1974
1986	N7	Report of the Commission on Social Welfare, July 1986
1992	N/10	Report of the Review Group on the Treatment of Households in the Social Welfare code

Social Security, Pensions

1976	N.3	A National Income Related Pension Scheme—A Discussion Paper
1978	N4	Social Insurance for the Self-Employed—A Discussion Paper
1987	N8	First Report of the National Pensions Board
1988	N9	Report on the Extension of Social Insurance to the Self-Employed. National Pensions Board
1988	N9/1	Report on the Tax Treatment of Occupational Pension Schemes. National Pensions Board
1989	N/09/02	Report on Equal Treatment for Men and Women in Occupational Pension Schemes. National Pensions Board

Itineracy

| 1983 | Z29 | Report of the Travelling People Review Body, February 1983 |

HEALTH

General: Insurance and Medical Services

1974	R.119	Restructuring the Department of Health. The Separation of Policy and Execution
1976	R.133	Report of the Working Party on Prescribing and Dispensing in the General Medical Service
1978	I 133/26	National Prices Commission Occasional Paper No. 27. Report on Irish Dental Laboratories
1984	Z 32	Report of the Working Party on the General Medical Service
1986	6/86	19th Report of the Dail Committee on Public Expenditure. The proposed Dublin Dental Hospital
1986	Z.34	Report Health Services, 1983–1986
1986	Z35	Nursing Homes in the Republic of Ireland. A Study of the Private and Voluntary Sector
1986	Z36	'It's Our Home': The Quality of Life in Private and Voluntary Nursing Homes
1989	Z/49	Report of the Commission on Health Funding

Particular Problems

1983	I178	Restrictive Practices Commission. Report of Enquiry into the Statutory Restrictions on the provision of Dental Prostheses 1982
1984	Z 30	Towards a Full Life. Green Paper on Services for Disabled People
1986	Z37	Communication Networks and the Elderly
1986	Z38	This is our World: Perspectives of some Elderly People on Life in Suburban Dublin
1987	Z42	Choices in Community Care: Day Centres for the Elderly in the Eastern Health Board
1988	Z45	National Council for the Aged 1988 Report No. 18. Caring for the Elderly. Part I: A study of careers at home and in the community
1988	Z46	The Years Ahead. A Policy for the Elderly. Report of the Working Party on Services for the Elderly
1988	Z47	Caring for the Elderly Part II. The Caring Process: A Study of Care in the Home
1989	Z/48	National Council for the Aged. Sheltered Housing in Ireland. Its Role and Contribution in the Care of the Elderly
1990	Z/50	Health—Peoples' Beliefs and Practices

Children's Services and Health Issues

1975	Z.21	Task Force on Child Care Services—Interim Report
1976	Z.22	Report of the Committee on Non-Accidental Injury to Children, March, 1976
1981	Z21/1	Task Force on Child Care Services Final Report
1984	Z 31	Adoption. Report of Review Committee on Adoption Services
1987	Z40	Children's Dental Health in Ireland in 1984
1988	Z44	Childhood Leukaemia in the Republic of Ireland: Mortality and Incidence. A Report Commissioned by the Department of Health
1989	I/198	The Internal Market for Toys. Toy Safety
1992	O/R 26/92	Report of the Special Committee on the Recognition of Foreign Adoptions Bill, 1990 24/4/91

Pharmaceutical Products, Drugs

1974	R.123	Report of the Committee on Drug Education, April, 1974
1976	31/76	Report of the Special Committee on the Misuse of Drugs Bill, 1973
1981	Z27	Report on the Review of Arrangements for the Supply of Drugs and Medicines
1987	Z39/1	National Co-Ordinating Committee on Drug Abuse. First Annual Report, June 1986

Mental Health

1973	Z.12	Psychiatric Nursing Services of Health Boards—Report of Working Party
1980	J85/1	Third Interim Report of the Interdepartmental Committee on Mentally Ill and Maladjusted Persons
1980	R143	Services for the Mentally Handicapped Report of a Working Party
1985	Z33	The Psychiatric Services—Planning for the Future
1991	Z/51	Needs and Abilities A Policy for the Intellectually Disabled Report of the Review Group on Mental Handicap Services July 1990
1992	Z.28	Report of the Inspector of Mental hospitals for the years 31st December 1988 and 1989
1992	Z/53	Green Paper On Mental Health

Professions

1974	Z.19	The General Practitioner in Ireland
1975	Z.20	Survey of Workload of Public Health Nurses. Report of Working Group appointed by the Minister for Health
1978	I 133/27	National Prices Commission Occasional Paper No. 29 Veterinary Practice in Ireland
1980	Z26	Working Party on General Nursing Report

EDUCATION

General Policy

1977	E.80	A Policy for Youth and Sport
1979	R140	Dept. of Education. School Transport Scheme. Report of Study carried out by Hyland Associates Limited. (Management and Research Consultants)
1980	E89	White Paper on Educational Development
1984	E95	Programme for Action in Education 1984–1987
1985	E101	Partners in Education. Serving Community Needs. Green Paper
1987	E104	Action Handbook—How to implement gender equality
1992	E/107	Education For A Changing World. Green Paper 1992

Primary and Secondary Education

| 1991 | E/106 | Report of the Primary Education Review Body |

Higher Education

| 1972 | E73 | The Higher Education Authority Report on University Reorganisation, July, 1972 |
| 1972 | E74 | The Higher Education Authority Report on the Ballymun Project, July, 1972 |

Adult Education

| 1973 | E.79 | Adult Education in Ireland |
| 1984 | E97 | Lifelong Learning. Report of the Commission on Adult Education |

Teachers: Training, Salaries

1980	E87	Review Body on Teachers' Pay Interim Report
1984	E99	Report of the Committee on In service Education

Specific Problems

1972	E75	The Education of Children who are Handicapped by Impaired Hearing
1973	E.78	Radioactive Substances and X–Rays in Schools
1979	E83	Effects of Competitive Sport on Young Children in Ireland
1982	E91	The Education of Physically Handicapped Children
1982	E92	Report of the Pupil Transfer Committee
1984	E96	The Education and Training of Severely and Profoundly Mentally Handicapped Children in Ireland
1985	E100	Report of the Committee on Discipline in Schools
1988	E105	Guidelines on Remedial Education

NATIONAL CULTURE

1978	E82	A Select List of Books on Ireland
1983	E93	Glass by Thomas and Richard Pugh in the National Museum of Ireland by: Catriona Mac Leod
1983	E94	The Natural History Museum, Dublin, by C. E. O'Riordan M. Sc. Ph.D.
1986	Y17	Report of the Committee concerned with the Outflow of Works of Art
1987	Y18	Access and Opportunity. A White Paper on Cultural Policy
1991	W/21A	Monuments in The Past. Photographs 1870–1936

The Irish Language

1972	F93/3	Implementing a Language Policy
1974	F.111	An Ghaeilge sa Choras Oideachais-Irish in Education
1976	R.131	Committee on Irish Language Attitudes Research-Report
1985	10/85	An Comhchoiste don Ghaeilge. An Chead Tuarascail faoi usaid na Gaeilge a leathadh in imeachtai na Dala agus an tSeanaid agus i dtimpeallacht an da Theach. Joint Committee on the Irish Language. First Report on the extension of the use of Irish in the proceedings of the Dail and Seanad and in the environs of the Houses
1986	9/86	Joint Committee on the Irish Language. Second Report on the extension of the use of Irish in the Proceedings of the Dail and Seanad and in the environs of both Houses

1986	14/86	Joint Committee on Irish Language. First Annual Report from the Joint Committee 1985/86
1988	2/88	First Report from the Second Joint Committee on the Irish Language
1988	8/88	Second Joint Committee on the Irish Language. Second Report. Recommendations regarding the Promotion of the Irish Language in the Houses of the Oireachtas and within the Political Parties
1988	9/88	Second Joint Committee on the Irish Language. Third Report from the Joint Committee—Survey amongst the Members of the Houses of the Oireachtas in connection with the Irish Language
1989	O/R/88/11	Second Joint Committee on the Irish Language. Fourth Report from the Joint Committee—Recommendations regarding advertising through the medium of the Irish Language
1989	O/R/88/12	The Second Joint Committee on the Irish Language. The Fifth Report from the Joint Committee: The Influence of Computerisation on the Irish Language

Newspapers, Broadcasting, Television and Cinema

1974	R.120	Broadcasting Review Committee Report, 1974
1977	I.133/22	National Prices Commission Occasional Paper No. 23. Radio Telefis Eireann Costs and Revenues—December 1976
1978	I 165	Restrictive Practices Commission. Report of Inquiry into the Supply and Distribution of Cinema Films
1983	I176	Restrictive Practices Commission Report of Enquiry into the supply and distribution of Daily and Sunday Newspapers published in Ireland, and of Newspapers, Periodicals and Magazines distributed by Wholesalers, 1979
1984	E98	Educational Broadcasting Committee. Report and Recommendations
1985	T29	Report of the Cable Systems Committee
1985	T31	Review of Radio Telefis Eireann, 1985. Report to the Minister for Communications by Stokes Kennedy Crowley, Management Consultants

LEGAL ADMINISTRATION, POLICE, LAW

Administration and Procedure

| 1972 | J.71/7 | Eleventh Interim Report of the Committee on Court Practice and Procedure |

1972	J.71/9	Thirteenth Interim Report of the Committee on Court Practice and Procedure. The Solicitor's Right of Audience
1972	J.71/10	Fourteenth Interim Report of the Committee on Court Practice and Procedure. Liability of Barristers and Solicitors for Professional Negligence
1972	J.71/11	Fifteenth Interim Report of the Committee on Court Practice and Procedure. On the Spot Fines
1972	J.71/12	Sixteenth Interim Report of the Committee on Court Practice and Procedure. The Jurisdiction of the Master of the High Court
1973	J.71/8	Twelfth Interim Report of the Committee on Court Practice and Procedure—Courts Organisation
1973	J.71/13	Seventeenth Interim Report of the Committee on Court Practice and Procedure—Court Fees
1973	J.71/14	Eighteenth Interim Report of the Committee on Court Practice and Procedure—Execution of Money Judgments, Orders and Decrees
1974	J.71/15	Nineteenth Interim Report on Court Practice and Procedure-Desertion and Maintenance
1974	R.121	Law Enforcement Commission Report
1978	J71/16	Twentieth Interim Report of the Committee on Court Practice and Procedure. Increase of Jurisdiction of the District Court and the Circuit Court
1978	J93	Committee on Civil Legal Aid and Advice Report to Minister for Justice
1981	J 98	Community Service Orders—a method of dealing with offenders brought before the courts
1983	J103	A Study of the Alcohol Education Court Programme
1987	4/87	Fifteenth Report of the Select Committee on Crime, Lawlessness and Vandalism. The Prosecution of Offenders
1989	J/114	Rules of the Superior Courts (No. 1), 1989. Guide to changes in the Rules of the Superior Courts 1986
1990	J/117	Report of Committee to Enquire into Certain Aspects of Criminal Procedure—March 1990

Police

1978	J94	Report of the Committee to Recommend certain Safeguards for Persons in Custody and for members of An Garda Siochana
1979	J95	Report of Garda Siochana Committee of Inquiry
1985	8/84	Fourth Report of the Select Committee on Crime, Lawlessness and Vandalism. Controls on the Private Security Industry

1985	9/84	Fifth Report of Select Committee on Crime, Lawlessness and Vandalism. Report on a visit to Scotland Yard
1986	4/86	Eighth Report of the Select Committee on Crime, Lawlessness and Vandalism. Safeguards for persons being questioned in Garda stations and for members of the Garda Siochana
1986	J109	Treatment of Persons in Custody in Garda Stations. Proposals for Regulations to be made by the Minister for Justice
1987	20/86	Fourteenth Report of the Select Committee on Crime, Lawlessness and Vandalism. Objectives of the Garda Siochana
1987	J112	Garda Training Committee. Report on Probationer Training
1992	O/R 09/92	Second Report of the Select Committee on Crime. The Further Civilianisation of An Garda Siochana

Prisons

1980	J97	Summary of Report prepared by The Irish National Council on Alcoholism on the Prevalence and Treatment of Problem Drinking among Prisoners
1983	J102	Drug Abusers in the Dublin Committal Prisons: A Survey
1985	J107	Report of the Committee of Inquiry into the Penal System. (Reprinted 1991)
1990	J/118	Scheme of Compensation for Personal Injuries Criminally Inflicted on Prison Officers
1991	J/120	Report of the Advisory Group on Prison Deaths

Juvenile Offenders

1975	J.84	First Interim Report of the Interdepartmental Committee on Mentally Ill and Maladjusted Persons. Assessment Services for the Courts in respect of Juveniles
1975	J.85	Second Interim Report of the Interdepartmental Committee on Mentally Ill and Maladjusted Persons. The Provision of Treatment for Juvenile Offenders and Potential Juvenile Offenders
1979	R139	A Report on the Law and Procedures regarding the prosecution and disposal of Young Offenders
1992	O/R 07/92	First Report of the Select Committee on Crime. Juvenile Crime: Its Causes and Its Remedies

Law

1972	1/72	Second Report of the Select Committee on Statutory Instruments. T.228

1973	R.118	Bankruptcy Law Committee Report
1974	J.83	Scheme of Compensation for Personal Injuries Criminally Inflicted
1976	M.76	The Law of Nullity in Ireland
1976	J.86	Report of the Advisory Committee on Law Reform; Reform of Law of Occupiers Liability in Ireland
1977	I.133/21	National Prices Commission Occasional Paper No. 22— Solicitors Remuneration in Ireland. December 1976
1980	J/96	Scheme of Civil Legal Aid and Advice
1984	1/84	First Report of the Select Committee on Crime, Lawlessness and Vandalism. Neighbourhood Watch as a Scheme for Community Involvement in Policing
1984	3/84	Joint Committee on Legislation. Report on Age of Majority
1984	4/84	Second Report of the Select Committee on Crime, Lawlessness and Vandalism. The role of Officers of Customs and Excise in controlling the supply of illegal drugs
1985	2/85	Sixth Report of Select Committee on Crime, Lawlessness and Vandalism. Confiscation of assets illegally acquired through drug trafficking
1985	11/85	Third Report of the Select Committee on Crime, Lawlessness and Vandalism. The decriminalisation of certain offences under the Vagrancy Acts
1985	J106	The Status of Children
1985	J108	Report of the Tribunal of Inquiry into 'The Kerry Babies Case'
1986	5/86	Ninth Report of the Select Committee on Crime Lawlessness and Vandalism. Report on certain offences under the Vagrancy Acts
1986	11/86	Tenth Report of the Select Committee on Crime Lawlessness and Vandalism. Controls on Video Nasties
1987	19/86	Thirteenth Report of the Select Committee on Crime, Lawlessness and Vandalism. Liability of Parents for Contributing to the Delinquency of their Children
1990	J/115	Report of the Committee on Fundraising Activities for Charitable and other Purposes
1990	J/116	Committee on Public Safety and Crowd Control—Report February 1990
1991	J/119	Report of the Stardust Victims Compensation Tribunal

Serials

Stationary Office Catalogue numbers for Serials have changed from time to time. Changes are noted when they fall within the period of this work 1972–1992. The reader should be aware that for the period 1922–1972 other catalogue numbers might have applied as well and the reader should consult Maltby and McKenna.

GOVERNMENT

Treaty Series	1930–	X.6
Indexes:		
Treaty Series 1978 No. 2: General index to the Treaty Series 1971–1976		
Treaty Series 1986 No. 11: Chronological index to the Treaty Series 1977–1986		
Public Service Advisory Council	1974–	F.120
State Directory (Directory of State Services 1966–1975)	1976–	F.72
Civil Service Commission	1977–	B.48
Returns of local taxation	1921/26–	K.2
Local authority estimates	1977–	K.116
Seirbhis Phoibli (Journal of the Department of the Public Service)	1980–	F.164
Developments in the European Communities	1973–	X.49
Deputy Keeper of the Public Records	1920–	J.27
Index to Iris Oifigiuil	1922–	M14

NATIONAL FINANCE

Budget	1958–	F.56
Economic background to the budget	1976–1987	F.125
Appropriation accounts	1922/23–1983	F.4
Appropriation accounts together with the	1984–1988	F.4
Report of the Comptroller and Auditor General		
Annual Report of the Comptroller and Auditor General and Appropriations Accounts	1989–	F.4
Estimates for public services	1922/23–	F.78
Finance Accounts	1922/23–	F.5
Revenue Commissioners	1923/24–	C.6
Statistical Report of the Revenue Commissioner	1989–	C.6
Public capital programme (Capital budget 1963–1974)	1963–	F.65
Customs and Excise Tariff	1923–	C.2

AGRICULTURE, FOOD, FORESTRY AND FISHERIES

Minister for Agriculture and Fisheries	1965/ 66–1976	A.1
Minister for Agriculture	1977–1986	A.1
Minister for Agriculture and Food	1987–	A.1
Irish Land Commissioners	1920/21–	L.1
Sea and Inland Fisheries	1926/28–1981	G.10
Forest and Wildlife Service	1933/38	L.57
	1984–1986	G.28
Minister for Fisheries and Forestry	1982–1984	G.10
Minister for the Marine	1985–	G.10

Forest Service Report	1987–1988	L.57
Ireland Forestry Operational Programme	1989–1993	L.57
Wildlife Service Report	1989–	G.28
Department of Agriculture and Fisheries Journal	1922–1976	A.2
Department of Agriculture Journal	1977	A.2
Irish fisheries investigations Series A (freshwater)	1966–	G.21
Irish fisheries investigations Series B (marine)	1967–	G.22
Veterinary Research Laboratory	1969/70– 1987/88	A.68
Veterinary Laboratory Service	1989–	

ECONOMIC POLICY: DEVELOPMENT, PLANNING AND TRADE

Statistical abstract of Ireland	1931–	U.74
National income and expenditure	1959–	U.1
Input-output tables	1964 1969 1975 1985	U.5
Household Budget Survey	1971–	U.104
Economic review and outlook	1976–	F.75
Census of population	1926 1936 1946 1951 1956 1961 1966 1971 1979 1981 1986 1991	U.40
The trend of employment and unemployment	1935/36–	U.2
Vital statistics	1953–	U.3
Companies	1922–	I.10

Assurance companies	1922–1985	I.18
Insurance Annual Report	1986–	
Irish Statistical Bulletin	to June, 1973	U.36
	Sept.73–Sept.86	U.37
Statistical Bulletin	Dec. 1986–	U.37
Examiner of Restrictive Practices	1972–	I.142
Restrictive Practices Commission	1974–1987	I.149
National Prices Commission	1971–1986	I.132
Mergers, Take-overs and Monopolies (Control) Act 1978. Report by the Minister for Industry and Commerce	1978/79–	I.171
Fair Trade Commission	1988–	I.149
Director of Consumer Affairs	1979–1987	I 170
Director of Consumer Affairs and Fair Trade	1988–	I 170
Trade statistics of Ireland	1930–	U.9
Registrar of Friendly Societies	1923–	I.23
Research and development in Ireland	1963 1967	I.150
	1969 1971	
	1974	
	1975	Y.4
Census of industrial production	1979–	U.112
Controller of Patents, Designs and Trade Marks	1966/67–	I.24
Census of distribution (Census of distribution and services 1966)	1933, 1951/54	U.78
	1956/59 1966	
	1971 1977	
Census of Services	1988	U.78

TRANSPORTATION, ENERGY AND THE ENVIRONMENT

Dept. of the Environment	1977–	K.24
Road Freight Transport Survey	1980–	U.110

POSTS AND TELEGRAPHS

Dept. of Posts and Telegraphs, Commercial accounts	1922/26–	F.24

LABOUR

Labour Court	1946/47–1987	V.93
	1988/89/90	V.97
Labour Force Survey	1975–	U.106
Labour Relations Commission	1991–	V.96
Department of Labour	1983–	V.94
Labour Inspection	1977–	V.1
Employment Appeals Tribunal	1977–	V.7

SOCIAL SECURITY

Statistical Information on Social Welfare Services	1983–	N.6
Guide to the social services (Irregular)	1941–	N.2
Dept. of Social Welfare	1947/49–	N.1
Appeal Office	1991–	N/11

HEALTH

National Health Council (Irregular)	1956/ 57–1986	Z.3
Perinatal Statistics	1984–	Z.43

| Statistical information relevant to the health services | 1976– 85 | Z.23 |
| Health Statistics | 1986– | Z.41 |

EDUCATION

Dept. of Education, Statistical report	1964/ 65–	E.6
List of National Schools	1954–	E.P.22
List of recognized Secondary schools	1954/ 55–	E.1.11
Oideas	1968–	E.62
Rules and programme for secondary schools	1924/ 25–	E.1.5
Universities and colleges: Accounts of receipts and expenditure of the National University of Ireland	1922/ 23–	F.10

NATIONAL CULTURE

| National Museum of Ireland, Board of Visitors | 1921/ 22– | E.2 |
| National Library of Ireland, Council of Trustees | 1921/ 22– | E.22 |

LEGAL ADMINISTRATION, POLICE, LAW

Prisons and places of detention	1928–	J.4
Register of prohibited publications	1931–1985	J.46
Censorship of Publications Board and Censorship of Publications Appeal Board	1946/1947–1976	J.60
Censorship of Publications Board	1980–1982	J.60
Crime, Commissioner of Garda Siochana (Police)	1947–	J.61
Criminal Injuries Compensation Tribunal	1974/75–	J.88
Commissioners of Charitable Donations and Bequests	1923–	J.12
Bord Uchtála (Adoption Board)	1953–	J.64

Publications of the National Economic and Social Council

1	Report on the Economy in 1973 and the Prospects for 1974	1974
2	Comments on Capital Taxation Proposals	1974
3	The Economy in 1974 and Outlook for 1975	1974
4	Regional Policy in Ireland A Review	1975
5	Population and Employment Projections: 1971–86	1975
6	Comments on the OECD Report on Manpower Policy in Ireland	1975
7	Jobs and Living Standards Projections and Implications	1975
8	An Approach to Social Policy	1975
9	Report on Inflation	1975
10	Causes and Effects on Inflation in Ireland	1975
11	Income Distribution: A Preliminary Report	1975
12	Education Expenditure in Ireland	1976
13	Economy in 1975 and Prospects for 1976	1975
14	Population Projections 1971–86: The Implications for Social Planning—Dwelling Needs	1976
15	The Taxation of Farming Profits	1976
16	Some Aspects of Finance for Owner-Occupied Housing	1976
17	Statistics for Social Policy	1976
18	Population Projections 1971–86: The Implications for Education	1976
19	Rural Areas: Social Planning Problems	1976
20	The Future of Public Expenditure in Ireland	1976
21	Report on Public Expenditure	1976
22	Institutional Arrangements for Regional Economic Development	1976
23	Report on Housing Subsidies	1977
24	A Comparative Study of Output, Value-Added and Growth in Irish and Dutch Agriculture	1976
25	Towards a Social Report	1977
26	Prelude to Planning	1976
27	New Farm Operators, 1971 to 1975	1977
28	Service-type Employment and Regional Development	1977
29	Some Major Issues in Health Policy	1977
30	Personal Incomes by County in 1973	1977
31	The Potential for Growth in Irish Tax Revenues	1977
32	The Work of the NESC: 1974–1976	1977
33	Comments on Economic and Social Development, 1976–1989	1977
34	Alternative Growth Rates in Irish Agriculture	1977

35   Population and Employment Projections 1986: A Reassessment   1977
36   Universality and Selectivity: Strategies in Social Policy   1978
37   Integrated Approaches to Personal Income Taxes and Transfers   1978
38   Universality and Selectivity: Social Services in Ireland   1978
39   The Work of the NESC: 1977   1978
40   Policies to Accelerate Agriculture Development   1978
41   Rural Areas: Change and Development   1978
42   Report on Policies for Agricultural and Rural Development   1978
43   Productivity and Management   1979
44   Comments on Development for Full Employment   1978
45   Urbanisation and Regional Development in Ireland   1979
46   Irish Forestry Policy   1979
47   Alternative Strategies for Family Income Support   1980
48   Transport Policy   1980
49   Enterprise in the Public Sector   1980
50   Major Issues in Planning Services for Mentally and Physically
     Handicapped Persons   1980
51   Personal Incomes by Region in 1977   1980
52   Tourism Policy   1980
53   Economic and Social Policy 1980–83: Aims and Recommendations   1980
54   The Future of the National Economic and Social Council   1981
55   Urbanisation: Problems of Growth and Decay in Dublin   1981
56   Industrial Policy and Development: A Survey of Literature from the
     Early 1960s to the Present   1981
57   Industrial Employment and the Regions 1960–82   1981
58   The Socio-Economic Position of Ireland within the European
     Economic Community   1981
59   The Importance of Infrastructure to Industrial Development in
     Ireland—Roads, Telecommunications and Water Supply   1981
60   Minerals Policy   1981
61   Irish Social Policies: Priorities for Future Development   1981
62   Economic and Social Policy 1981—Aims and Recommendations   1981
63   Population and Labour Force Projections by County and Region,
     1987–1991   1982
64   A Review of Industrial Policy (A Summary of this report is
     available separately)   1982
65   Farm Incomes   1982
66   Policies for Industrial Development: Conclusions and
     Recommendations   1982
67   An Analysis of Job Losses in Irish Manufacturing Industry   1983
68   Social Planning in Ireland: Its Purposes and Organisational
     Requirements   1983
69   Housing Requirements and Population Change, 1981–1991   1983
70   Economic and Social Policy 1982: Aims and Recommendations   1983

71 Education: The Implications of Demographic Change   1984
72 Social Welfare: The Implications of Demographic Change   1984
73 Health Services: The Implications of Demographic Change   1984
74 Irish Energy Policy   1984
75 Economic and Social Policy 1983: Aims and Recommendations.
    A Review of the Implications of Recent Demographic Changes
    for Education, Social Welfare and the Health Services
    (Background Paper)   1984
76 The Role of Financial System in Financing the Traded Sectors   1984
77 The Criminal Justice System: Policy and Performance   1985
78. Information for Policy   1985
79 Economic and Social Policy Assessment   1985
80 The Financing of Local Authorities   1985
81 Designation of Areas for Industrial Policy   1985
82 Manpower Policy in Ireland   1986
83 A Strategy for Development 1986–1990 (A Summary of this report
    is available separately)   1986
84 Community Care Service: An Overview   1987
85 Redistribution Through State Social Expenditure in the Republic of
    Ireland: 1973–1980   1988
86 The Nature and Functioning of Labour Markets   1988
87 A Review of Housing Policy   1989
88 Ireland in the European Community: Performance, Prospects and
    Strategy   1989
89 A Strategy for the Nineties: Economic Stability and Structural
    Change   1990
90 The Economic and Social Implications of Emigration   1991
91 Women's Participation in the Irish Labour Market   1992
92 The Impact of Reform of the Common Agricultural Policy   1992
93 The Irish Economy in a Comparative Institutional Perspective   1993
94 The Association between Economic Growth and Employment
    Growth in Ireland   1993

Index

adoption 36, 48
adult education 37
Advertising 20, 28, 29, 39
Aer Lingus 17
Aer Rianta 16, 18
AFT/ACOT 23
aged, the 35
Agricultural Credit Corporation 16
agricultural developments 15, 20
agricultural education 23
agriculture 19, 20, 21, 23, 25, 44, 45, 49, 50, 51
air services 16, 21
Air/Sea Rescue 32
airport 16, 18
alcohol 40
America 16
American Loan Counterpart Fund 14, 15
An Post 17, 18
Anglo-Irish Agreement 16
aquaculture 21
army 13
art 20, 38
atomic energy 22
audit 13
Auditor General 13, 44

B and I Line 16, 17
Ballymun project 37
bankruptcy 42
barristers 40
benefits 22
bequests 48
bi-lateral aid 16
bogs 25
books 38
Bord na gCon 17, 18
Bord Na Mona 16, 17, 25

Bord Telecom 17
Bord Uchtala 48
borough 14
bovine tuberculosis 24
broadcasting 39
budget 18, 20, 23, 44
building land 25
building societies 28
buildings 26
business 22, 25
bye-elections 11

cable television 29, 39
capital projects 23
capital taxation 49
catering 25
censorship 48
census of distribution 46
census of industrial production 46
census of population 45
census of services 46
Central Statistics Office 13
charitable donations 48
chemicals 19, 21, 22
child care 33, 36
children 33, 36, 38, 42
CIE 17, 27
cinema 39
Circuit Court 40
civil legal aid 40, 42
civil servants 14, 33
Civil Service 13
Civil Service Commission 12, 43
climate 31
clothing 21, 22
co-operation, North-South 15, 22
co-operation with developing countries 16
coal 28

Common Agricultural Policy 20, 51
communications 30, 35
community care 51
company taxation 19, 22
compensation 42
competition 22, 29
competitiveness 25
comptroller 13, 44
computer and computerisation 13, 39
Conference on Security and
    Cooperation 16
construction 12, 21, 22, 25, 26
consumer 21, 27, 46
Consumer Councils 27
consumer education 27
contracts 12
Coras Iompair Eireann 17, 27
costs 12, 25
County Borough Council 14
county 14, 49, 50
court 39, 40, 41
credit 18, 21, 25
crime 40, 41, 42, 48
criminal injuries 42, 48
criminal justice 40, 51
criminal procedure 40, 41
culture 20, 38
Customs and Excise 19, 20, 21, 42, 44

Dail 11, 12, 23, 24, 27, 32, 35, 38
Dail Constituency Commission 13
Dail elections 11
Dail procedure 12, 38
debt 23
decimal currency 23
defence 13
defence forces 13
demographic change 51
dental 19
dental services 19, 35, 36
departments 13
designs 46
developing countries 16
development 16, 50, 51
disabled people 35, 36
discrimination vs. women 33
disease 20, 24, 36
distribution 25, 28, 29, 39

division of Ireland 15
drainage 31
drink 22, 27, 28, 41
drug education 36
drugs 36, 41, 42
Dublin 14, 24, 29, 32, 35, 50
Dun Laoghaire Harbour 32
dwelling needs 49

earnings 25
EC Parliament 18
economic development 29, 49, 51
economic growth 51
economic policy 15, 22, 30, 50, 51
economic structure 15, 20, 51
economy 45, 49, 51
education 16, 20, 32, 33, 37, 38, 39,
    40, 48, 49, 51
EEC 18
effluents 31
elderly 35
elections 11, 14, 18
Electoral Area Boundaries
    Commission 14
electoral procedures 11
electors 11
electrical goods 25
Electricity Supply Board 17, 31
electricity 31
electronics 22
emigration 51
employment 13, 20, 21, 29, 33, 45, 47,
    49, 50, 51
energy 15, 20, 30, 31, 51
engineering 22, 25, 29
enterprise 50
environment 30, 31, 47
equal opportunity 21, 33
equality 18, 19, 33, 34
European Assembly 22
European Communities 18, 21, 22, 43
European Community 18, 20, 21, 51
European Economic Community 22, 50
European Monetary System 22
European Union 21, 22
Evergreen Export Bank 19
excise 21
expenditure 45, 49, 51

Fair Trade Commission 22, 28, 46
family income 50
farm records 23
farms and farming 19, 49, 50
fees 40
fertilizer 18, 25
finance 13, 14, 21, 23, 44, 49, 51
financial condition 17
financial procedures 22
financial resources 21
financial services 22, 30, 51
fines 40
fire service 14
fisheries 19, 21, 24, 44, 45
flour industry 27
food 21, 22, 23, 26, 44
food and drink industry 22, 30
footwear 22
footwear industry 22, 24
forests and Forestry 18, 20, 24, 44, 45, 50
Forum for a New Ireland 15
freight haulage 32
freight transport 47
fruit and vegetables 24
full employment 29, 50
furniture 24
furniture industry 24

Gaeltachta 17
Gais Eireann 17
Garda Siochana 40, 41, 48
gender equality 33, 37
General Election 11
government contracts 12
government 11, 12, 14
grant distribution 14
grocery 28, 29
growth rates 49

Hackney 25, 32
handicapped 33, 36, 50
handicapped children 38
health 20, 22, 34, 35, 47, 49
Health Department 35, 48
Health Services 35, 36, 37, 48, 51
High Court 40

higher education 37, 48
horses 17, 18, 25
hospitals 35, 36
Household Budget 45
household incomes 22
housing 27, 35, 49, 50, 51

income and incomes 22, 49, 50
income distribution 49, 51
industrial concentration 28
Industrial Credit Corp 16
industrial development 29, 30, 50
industrial development agencies 30
Industrial Development Authority 13
industrial failure 30
industrial performance 26, 29, 50
industrial policy 21, 29, 50, 51
industrial production 46
industrial progress 24, 25, 30
industrial promotion 30
industrial relations 34
industrial training 30
industry 22, 25, 26, 29, 30, 50
inflation 49
information 26, 51
infrastructure 21, 32, 50
injuries 36, 41, 42
innovation 26
input-output tables 45
insurance 19, 21, 25, 28, 46
International Relations 14
investment 29
Iris Oifigiuil 43
Irish language 38, 39
Irish Life Assurance 17
Irish Meteorological Service 31
Irish National Petroleum Company 17
Irish National Stud Company 17, 18
Irish Shipping Limited 16, 17
Irish Steel Limited 17
iron 28

job losses 50
juvenile offenders 41
juveniles 41

Kerry Babies Case 42

labour 34, 47, 51
labour court 47
labour force 33, 47, 50, 51
labour markets 21, 51
land 23, 25
Land Commissioners 44
land structure reform 23
language 20, 38, 39
law 29, 34, 40, 41, 42
legal administration 39, 40, 41, 42, 48
legal aid 40
legal profession 29, 40, 42
legal systems 15
legislation 18
liabilitly 19, 21, 40, 42
library 14
licenses 19
living standards 49
local elections 11, 14
local government 12, 14, 27, 31, 43, 51
lottery 17, 18

maladjusted persons 36
management 33, 50
managers 33
manpower 33
manpower policy 33, 49, 51
manufacturing 25, 50
marine 44
marital breakdown 32, 33
marketing 20, 23
markets 19, 21, 23, 25
marriage 32
measurements 21
meat 18, 19, 20, 24
media 32
medical services 27, 35, 37
mental health 36
mentally ill 36, 41, 50
merchant marine 32
mergers 19, 20, 28, 46
migration 20
milk 19, 20, 24
Monetary Cooperation Fund 18
Monetary Union 20
money 23, 40
motor fuels 27, 29

motor insurance 25, 28
motor spirit 28
motor vehicles 18, 19, 25
museums 38, 48

National Archives 34
National Building Agency 16
National Council for the Aged 35
National Council on Alcoholism 41
National Development 29
National Economic and Social Council 49–51
National Health Council 47
National History Museum 38
National Income 34, 45
National Library of Ireland 48
National Lottery 17, 18
National Museum of Ireland 38, 48
National Partnership 29
National Prices Commission 24, 25, 27, 35, 37, 39, 46
National Science Council 26, 31
National Statistics Board 13
National University of Ireland 48
NESC 49–51
New Ireland Forum 15
newspapers 39
Northern Ireland Executive 14
Northern Ireland 14, 15
nullity, law of 42
nursing homes 35

OECD 49
Oideas 48
oil 20
Oireachtas 15, 39

parliament 12, 13, 18
patents 46
peatlands 26
penal system 41
pensions 34
perinatal 47
personal income 49, 50
pesticides 23
petroleum 17, 20
pharmaceutical products 22

physically handicapped 50
planning 15, 22, 29, 30, 49
police 40, 41
polling 11
pollution 18, 19, 20, 21, 31
population 33, 49, 50
Posts and Telegraphs 27, 47
poultry 19
poverty 21
power 31
presidency 22
presidential elections 11, 12
prices 19, 27, 29, 31
primary education 37
prison deaths 41
prison officers 41
prisoners 41
prisons 41, 48
private enterprises 27, 35
privatisation 30
procedure 12
production 23
productivity 50
Prohibited Publications 48
psychiatric services 36, 41
public capital programme 44
public debt 23
Public Expenditure 12, 13, 23, 24, 27, 32, 35, 49, 51
public health 37
Public Library 14
public safety 42
public sector 13, 14, 27, 50
public service and services 12, 13, 43, 44

Radio Telefis Eireann 16, 39
Rate Support 14
Reagan, Ronald 15
recovery 29
referenda 11, 12
reform 12, 14, 19
regional development 49, 50
regional policy 49
regions 50
Reifrinn 12
remedial education 38

remuneration 13, 14, 42
research 20, 23
research and development 21, 26, 31, 46
resource allocation 26
restrictive practices 22, 28, 29, 35, 39, 46
retail trade 20, 25, 28, 29
Revenue Commissioners 44
roads 18, 21, 32, 47, 50
rural areas 49, 50

safety 20, 34, 36
salaries 13, 14, 42
schools 37, 38, 48
science policy 26
science 26
scientists 26
Seanad Eireann 11, 38
securities 19, 20, 21
security industry 40
security 13, 16
self-employed 34
senate 11, 38
services sector 25, 49
services 27
sexual violence 33
Shannon Free Airport Development Company 29
sheep 18, 20, 24
shipping 16, 17, 20
shirtmaking 24
small business and Small businesses 25, 26
social planning 49, 50
social policy 29, 49, 50, 51
social security 19, 20, 34, 47
social services 34, 47, 50
social welfare 34, 47, 51
solicitors 28, 40, 42
sport 37, 38
standards 13
State Directory 13, 43
state-sponsored Bodies 16, 17, 18
statistical abstract 45
statistics 27, 46, 47, 48
status of women 18, 32, 33
statutory instruments 18, 19, 20, 21, 41

steel 17, 28
strikes 34
Subsistence Rates 14
superannuation 14

Taoiseach 12
tariffs and quotas 18, 19, 20, 21, 24
taxes and taxation 14, 19, 20, 22, 23,
   30, 34, 43, 49, 50
taxis 25, 32
teachers 38
teaching 20
technical 26
technology 26, 31
telecommunications 50
Telefis Eireann 16, 39
television 39
textile 21, 22, 24
Toghchain Uachtaráin, presidential
   elections 12
tour operators 28
tourism 22, 25, 27, 28, 50
toxic waste 19
toys 36
trade marks 46
trade 46
training 13, 30, 33, 38, 41
transfer of votes 11, 14
transfers 50
transport 15, 19, 20, 22, 31, 32, 37, 47,
   50
travel trade 28
travelling people 34
treaty 22, 43

unemployment 27, 45
United Kingdom 14, 29, 32

United States 15, 16
urbanisation 19, 50
utilities 32

vagrancy 42
value-added 49
value-added tax 20, 22
vandalism 40
vegetables 24
veterinary 37, 45
veterinary medicine 20, 37, 45
video 42
video nasties 42
violence 15, 33
vital statistics 45
votes 11

waste 20, 21
wastelands 26
water pollution 18, 20, 31
water quality 31, 50
water supply 50
Whiddy Island 31
white paper 13, 21, 22, 23, 27, 29, 33,
   37, 38
wildlife 44, 45
women 18, 32, 33, 51
women's rights 32, 33
woolen industry 24
work 20, 33, 34
work services 33
worker participation 30, 34

young children 33
young offenders 41
young workers 19, 21, 33
youth 20, 33, 37